The Hat

John Escott

Easystart

Series Editors: Andy Hopkins and Jocelyn Potter

1.1 What's the book about?

Work with a friend and talk about hats.

1 Do many people in your country have hats? Are they old people or young people?
2 Do you have a hat? Why (not)?
3 Do you like hats? Why (not)?

1.2 What happens first?

Look at the picture on page 1. Circle the right answer.

1 What country is this?
   a France.
   b The United States.
   c Italy.

2 What town is it?
   a New York.
   b Rome.
   c Paris.

3 Is it a good day for a walk?
   a Yes, but it's cold.
   b No, it's raining.
   c Yes, but it's hot.

4 How old is the man?
   a About twenty years old.
   b About thirty years old.
   c About forty years old.

5 What is he looking at?
   a A green and blue hat.
   b A red and yellow hat.
   c A green and yellow hat.

B ernardo lives in Rome. He likes hats. One day he is at a street
market near the Colosseum. Suddenly, he stops.

"I like *that* hat!" he says.

Bernardo buys the hat.

"I can put it in a bag for you," the woman says.

"No, it's OK," Bernardo says. "I can **wear** it. Put my old hat in
the bag, please."

market /ˈmɑrkɪt/ (n) I buy fruit in the *market,* not in a store.
wear /wɛr/ (v) I only *wear* this coat on very cold days.

Bernardo arrives home.

"Hello, Natalie," he says to his **wife**. "Do you like my new hat?"

Natalie looks at him. She thinks, "No!" But she says, "Why do you want **another** hat, Bernardo? You have twenty!"

"I like hats," Bernardo says. "And I like *this* hat."

Natalie sees some people in the street. "They're **laughing** at Bernardo's hat," she thinks. "What can I do with it?"

wife /waɪf/ (n) She is my sister, not my *wife*.
another /əˈnʌðər/ (det) Can I have *another* drink, please?
laugh /læf/ (v) I am *laughing* at the movie, not at you!

Two days later, Natalie takes the hat to a store. The store buys and **sells clothes**. The man in the store buys Bernardo's hat.

That afternoon, Bernardo looks for his hat.

"I can't find my hat, Natalie," he says.

He looks in every room of the house.

"*I* can buy you a new hat, Bernardo," Natalie says. She smiles. "Let's go to the store!"

sell /sɛl/ (v) He *is selling* his old car. He wants a new car.
clothes /kloʊz, kloʊðz/ (n) I never buy new *clothes*. This shirt is very old.

Three days later, Anna buys the hat.

Anna is a student from the United States. She is in Rome on vacation.

"I love this hat!" she thinks. She smiles. "I can get some **flowers** for it."

flowers /ˈflaʊɚz/ (n) There are some beautiful *flowers* in the backyard.

A week later, Anna gets an airplane home.

She lives in California, near the ocean.

That weekend, she goes down to the **harbor**. She goes to a **café** for a drink.

harbor /ˈhɑrbə/ (n) Is that your father's boat in the *harbor*?
café /kæˈfeɪ, kə-/ (n) They make good coffee in this *café*.

Mitch is sitting in the café, too. He sees Anna's hat.
"Who's under that hat?" Mitch thinks.

Anna looks up and sees him.

"Hi," Mitch says. "I love your hat."

"Thank you," Anna says. She smiles.

I'm Mitch," Mitch says.

"I'm Anna," Anna says. She thinks, "I like him. Maybe this is a **lucky** hat!"

lucky /ˈlʌki/ (adj) Seven is my *lucky* number.

Mitch moves to Anna's table. They talk about books and movies. Anna **tells** Mitch about Rome.

"It's a good place for hats!" she says.

Mitch laughs. "A beautiful hat for a beautiful girl," he says.

"Thank you," she says.

"Come to the movies with me tomorrow, Anna," Mitch says.

"OK," Anna says. "Why not?"

tell /tɛl/ (v) He *tells* good stories about his years in India.

2.1 Were you right?

Look at your answers to Activity 1.2 on page ii. Then finish the sentences with the words in the box.

hot   twenty   green and yellow   Rome   Italian

Bernardo is about ....*twenty*......... years old. He is
.... and he lives in ....*Rome*.................. .
He sees a beautiful .... hat and he wants it. It
is summer now and the sun is very ....*hot*.................. .

2.2 What more did you learn?

What comes first? Write 1–6. Then answer the questions.

( ) **a** Anna buys the hat.
What does she put on the hat?

....

( ) **b** Natalie takes the hat to a store and sells it.
What does Bernardo do?

....

(1) **c** Bernardo arrives home with his new hat.
How many hats does Bernardo have now?
Twenty-one...

( ) **d** Anna tells Mitch about Rome.
Does Mitch like Anna?

....

( ) **e** Anna takes an airplane home.
Where in the United States does Anna live?

....

( ) **f** Mitch moves to Anna's table.
What do they talk about?

....

2.3 Language in use

Look at the sentences on the right. Then finish the sentences about the pictures.

> They**'re laughing** at Bernardo's hat.
>
> Mitch **is sitting** in the café, too.

1 Natalie ....*is looking*.................... at Bernardo's new hat.

2 People .... at Bernardo's hat.

3 Natalie .... a new hat for Bernardo.

4 Anna .... a book on the airplane.

5 Anna .... a drink at the café.

6 Mitch and Anna ....

2.4 What happens next?

What do you think? Talk about the story and write notes.

Notes

Anna

Mitch

The hat

Suddenly, the **wind** takes Anna's hat away.

"My hat!" Anna says.

The wind **blows** the hat out across the water.

"It's OK," Mitch says. "Can I buy you a new hat? Do you know a store near here?"

"Yes, I do," Anna says. "Thank you."

She smiles at Mitch.

wind /wɪnd/ (n) Look at the trees! There's a strong *wind* today.
blow /bloʊ/ (v) He *is blowing* on his hot coffee.

It is early morning on a **beach** near the café.

Cal sleeps on the beach with Sunny, his **dog**. Cal has no money and no home. Every day, he plays his **guitar** on the street.

"Look, Sunny," he says. "A hat. Go and get it!"

beach /biːtʃ/ (n) Let's go to the *beach* for a swim.
dog /dɒg/ (n) I walk every day with my *dog*.
guitar /gɪˈtɑr/ (n) She plays beautiful music on her *guitar*.

Cal plays his guitar on the street that morning.

Many people stop and listen. They put money in the hat.

"Look at this money, Sunny!" Cal says. "This is a lucky hat! We can eat at the café today. And tomorrow!"

That night, a man comes to the beach. His name is Rod. He sees Cal and Sunny.

He sees the hat, too, and smiles.

"That's a good hat," he thinks.

He walks quietly across the beach. He takes the hat, then he walks away quickly.

In the morning, Cal says to Sunny, "Where's my lucky hat?"

3.1 Were you right?

Look at your answers to Activity 2.4. Then check (✓) the right answers here.

1 What takes Anna's hat away?

◯ **a** a boat   ◯ **b** the wind

2 Where do Cal and Sunny sleep?

◯ **a** on the beach   ◯ **b** in a hotel

3 Where does Cal play his guitar?

◯ **a** in a café   ◯ **b** on the street

4 What do people put in Cal's hat?

◯ **a** money   ◯ **b** food

5 What does Rod take?

◯ **a** the hat   ◯ **b** the guitar

3.2 What more did you learn?

Who is thinking? Write the letter.

3.3 Language in use

Look at the sentences in the box. Then look at the picture and answer the questions.

> Cal **sleeps** on the beach.
>
> Every day, he **plays** his guitar on the street.

1 What does Cal do every day?

   He ....plays............ (play) his guitar.

2 Where does he sit and play?

   He .... (sit) on the street.

3 What do people do?

   People .... (stop) and .... (listen) to him.

4 Do people give him money?

   Some people .... (put) money into the hat.

5 What does Sunny do?

   Sunny .... (sit) and .... (watch) the hat.

3.4 What happens next?

What do you think? Talk to your friends and write _Yes_ or _No_.

1 Cal finds Rod and the hat.   ....

2 Rod wears the hat.   ....

3 Rod gives the hat to a friend.   ....

4 Cal tells the police about the hat.   ....

5 Anna sees Rod with the hat.   ....

6 Another person finds the hat.   ....

Later that night, Rod goes into town.
He goes to a store. He has a **gun**.

"What do you want?" the woman in the store asks.

"Give me the money!" Rod says. "Quickly!"

"OK, OK," the woman says.

Rod takes the money and runs from the store.

The woman calls the police. "He's tall and thin," she says. "And he's wearing a green and yellow hat."

gun /gʌn/ (n) The policemen at the airport have *guns*.

Later, two policemen see Rod on the street.

"He's wearing a green and yellow hat!" one policeman says.

"And he's tall and thin!" his friend says. "It's him!"

Suddenly, Rod sees them. He runs.

"It's this hat," he thinks. "It isn't a lucky hat!"

He **throws away** the hat.

throw away /ˌθroʊ əˈweɪ/ (v) I *am throwing away* the old newspapers, not today's.

The hat falls into a taxi. A young woman, Gina, is in the taxi.
She laughs. "That's lucky!" she thinks. "I can wear this hat."
The taxi arrives at Los Angeles airport.
"Are you going on vacation?" the taxi driver asks Gina.
"No, I'm going home to Italy," Gina answers.

A day later, Gina is in Rome.

"It's a beautiful **city**," she thinks. "And it's *my* city."

A man stops and looks at her hat. Gina sees him.

"Do you like hats?" Gina asks him.

"I *love* hats!" Bernardo says.

city /ˈsɪti/ (n) Many people live and work in the *city* of London.

Talk to one or two friends. Put the pictures in order, 1–5. Then tell the story.

Now write five sentences about the people and the hat. How do they get the hat? What do they do with it?

1 ....

....

2 ....

....

3 ....

....

4 ....

....

5 ....

....

1 Work with two or three friends. Look at the hats. Who wears them?
Why do people wear them?

2 **Now look at this hat. You can drink from it!**

Work with your friends. What do you want from a hat? Do you want a hat with a TV or a telephone? Talk about it. Then design your hat and draw a picture.

3 **Tell the students in your class about your hat. What is it? When can you wear it? Why?**